D1541652

[ WARDRAW ]

3 1526 04628773 3

# SUPER CUTE!

# Baby Squirrels

by Megan Borgert-Spaniol

BLASTOFF! READERS

Note to Librarians, Teachers, and Parents:

**Blastoff! Readers** are carefully developed by literacy experts and combine standards-based content with developmentally appropriate text.

**Level 1** provides the most support through repetition of high-frequency words, light text, predictable sentence patterns, and strong visual support.

**Level 2** offers early readers a bit more challenge through varied simple sentences, increased text load, and less repetition of high-frequency words.

**Level 3** advances early-fluent readers toward fluency through increased text and concept load, less reliance on visuals, longer sentences, and more literary language.

**Level 4** builds reading stamina by providing more text per page, increased use of punctuation, greater variation in sentence patterns, and increasingly challenging vocabulary.

**Level 5** encourages children to move from "learning to read" to "reading to learn" by providing even more text, varied writing styles, and less familiar topics.

Whichever book is right for your reader, Blastoff! Readers are the perfect books to build confidence and encourage a love of reading that will last a lifetime!

This edition first published in 2016 by Bellwether Media, Inc.

No part of this publication may be reproduced in whole or in part without written permission of the publisher. For information regarding permission, write to Bellwether Media, Inc., Attention: Permissions Department, 5357 Penn Avenue South, Minneapolis, MN 55419.

Library of Congress Cataloging-in-Publication Data

Borgert-Spaniol, Megan, 1989- author.
Baby Squirrels / by Megan Borgert-Spaniol.
  pages cm. – (Blastoff! Readers. Super Cute!)
Summary: "Developed by literacy experts for students in kindergarten through grade three, this book introduces baby squirrels to young readers through leveled text and related photos"– Provided by publisher.
Audience: Ages 5-8
Audience: K to grade 3
Includes bibliographical references and index.
ISBN 978-1-62617-220-3 (hardcover: alk. paper)
1. Squirrels–Infancy–Juvenile literature. I. Title. II. Series: Blastoff! Readers. 1, Super Cute!
QL666.L245B67 2016
599.36–dc23

2015009720

Text copyright © 2016 by Bellwether Media, Inc. BLASTOFF! READERS and associated logos are trademarks and/or registered trademarks of Bellwether Media, Inc. SCHOLASTIC, CHILDREN'S PRESS, and associated logos are trademarks and/or registered trademarks of Scholastic Inc.

Printed in the United States of America, North Mankato, MN.

# Table of **Contents**

# Squirrel Kits!

Baby squirrels are called kits. There are 2 to 8 kits in a **litter**.

# In a Nest

Some litters live in leaf nests. The kits cuddle up inside.

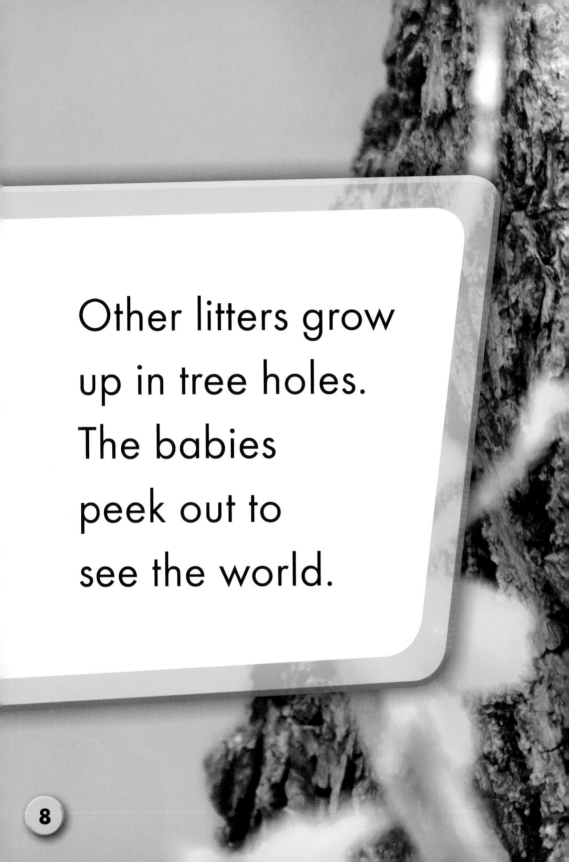

Other litters grow
up in tree holes.
The babies
peek out to
see the world.

A mom may
move her kits to
keep them safe.
She carries them
in her mouth.

## Time to Explore

Kits stay in their nest for about eight weeks. Then they start to explore outside.

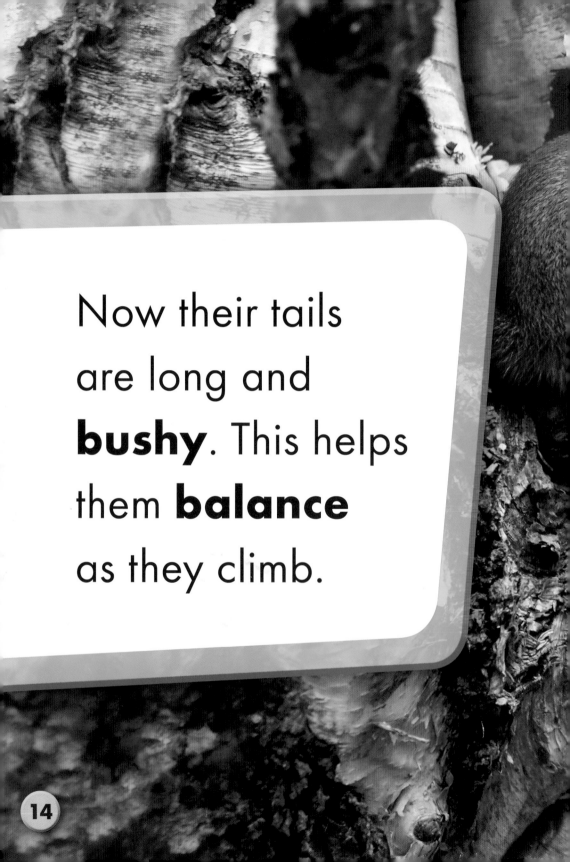

Now their tails are long and **bushy**. This helps them **balance** as they climb.

The babies love to play. They **wrestle** and chase one another.

The kits no longer **nurse**. They chew on nuts, seeds, and other foods.

This kit found
a tasty acorn.
Crunch away,
little squirrel!

# Glossary

**balance**—to stay steady and not fall

**bushy**—very thick

**litter**—a group of babies that are born together

**nurse**—to drink mom's milk

**wrestle**—to fight in a playful way

# To Learn More

## AT THE LIBRARY

Lloyd-Jones, Sally. *Just Because You're Mine.* New York, N.Y.: Harper, 2012.

Tafuri, Nancy. *The Busy Little Squirrel.* New York, N.Y.: Simon & Schuster Books for Young Readers, 2007.

Zobel, Derek. *Squirrels.* Minneapolis, Minn.: Bellwether Media, 2011.

## ON THE WEB

Learning more about squirrels is as easy as 1, 2, 3.

1. Go to www.factsurfer.com.

2. Enter "squirrels" into the search box.

3. Click the "Surf" button and you will see a list of related web sites.

With factsurfer.com, finding more information is just a click away.

# Index

The images in this book are reproduced through the courtesy of: Robert Eastman, front cover; Martha Marks, pp. 4-5; Albert Visage/ FLPA, pp. 6-7; George Jones, pp. 8-9; Minden Pictures/ Superstock, pp. 10-11; ZUMA Press/ Alamy, pp. 12-13; Julie DeRoche/ Glow Images, pp. 14-15; Yukihiro Fukuda/ Nature Picture Library, pp. 16-17; Allan Oman/ Glow Images, pp. 18-19; Frank Hecker/ Alamy, pp. 20-21.